JUST BE
and let the magic unfold
By
Sneha Pardikar

Copyright © 2023 by Sneha Pardikar

All rights reserved.

No part of this book may be

reproduced in any form without prior written

permission from the Author.

To get permission contact :

infinitemagicalbutterfly@gmail.com

ISBN : 9783758318139

Production and publishing:

BoD - Books on Demand, Norderstedt

Thank you Universe

We might have heard and read the topics that I have written in this book several times before through several resources. What this book says will be through the energy that I have felt and experienced. I thank all the beings who have in all possible ways given me the insight towards the ultimate truth which is and will always be : Life is a journey which can be experienced to its fullest by living it as it is.

Use this book as your go to option whenever the external factors stop you from "Just being".

Read it for your benefit and not as an escape tool for procrastination.

It is meant for the day to day chatter that goes in our mind and to actually address them.

Life is to live but we often misunderstand the meaning of the word "live".

This is my little attempt to give the "Living" a new meaning.

Let us get started

THE WAY IS HERE

Why is it, that when we try to apply the positive concepts, the rules of happiness, we often find out that it is not working as expected ?

How is it, that even after listening to most of the motivational ideas, the effect is still short lived?

We have heard, that the longer you hold a thought it starts to manifest, that life is beautiful, that it is better to let go and forget, that you are a go getter, to stay positive, the law of creating what we want which in other words is law of manifestation, also that what happens to us is all because of our karma, that we should flow like water, we should become the observer……..

All of the above mentioned is true but how to get to this point or how to attract this towards us, so that it will change the current state of our being?

Something to think about isn't it?

Well could there be a gap between the point where we are…. to the point where we want to see ourselves ?

And the answer is YES.

Imagine walking along one side of the river(Point A),now we see a lot of pleasant activities that are happening on the other side of the river(Point C). How to get to Point C?

The answer is using Point B. In this example 'Point B' could be a boat that helps us to cross over and reach point C. Basically a means of transport that will take us there.

Now if we associate this with our life, then what is this Point B?

Point A.....................**Point B**.....................Point C

The art of allowing oneself to just be in the state that one currently is, until one feels comfortable enough to feel differently.

The unfolding of magic begins. Have you had those friends, relatives or known personalities who have expressed their fear and nervousness or unpreparedness before exams, stage performances, interviews and they end up excelling in it? While you thought that this was their strategy (Exceptions excluded), what actually happened was, they felt the feeling of being nervous or anxious (or any emotion) without resisting it. They expressed it out. So now when the time came to perform, their body and mind were not blocked by this emotion and rather had enough space to allow them to be in the moment and give their best.

If they had allowed their logical limitation to pretend as if they are OK and if they had not expressed it out, these feelings would have been with them throughout their performance and would have given them an average outcome.

No matter how much we brain wash ourselves to feel grateful in life and be thankful for what we have, most of the times it exists only at the theory level because we do not feel it.

The amazing side effect of **just being** is that one constantly keeps emptying the storage tank of emotions which gives room for the body and mind to align and enhance the presence of mind. It helps to actually see and feel every moment of life in a more alive manner because mind is not occupied anymore in resisting the state of true feeling and there comes a moment when ideas start flowing through which we had never imagined before.

Those ideas could be anything from buying a pencil to making changes in the house, moving furniture and clearing up the living space and can even go up to investing time, money, energy for something. It could even be about eating a particular food item, watching a particular podcast or reading a particular book or article. And when this idea gets implemented, it actually turns out to be the solution for the problem that had made that person feel a certain way. Now when such a thing is experienced where solutions come in the form of random ideas to do certain things, then the mind, heart and soul will automatically start feeling grateful and thankful for those ideas because one knows how difficult it was to go through that tough phase and what magic this idea gave and one will 100% feel that this cannot be their thought process and that only some divine powers can deliver such ideas. Now without even intentionally planning the 5 minute of Gratitude routine, it happened automatically. Why? because we kept addressing the things that bother us right then and there without resisting the feeling. So once we have felt the awkward emotions for enough amount of time, the body and mind now automatically gets into the healing state and focus gets shifted naturally and in fact the person will also start to feel grateful and thankful for what they currently have.

Now the statement " The solution comes from within" or " There is not a single problem which does not have a solution" or "The solution / answer is right in front of us" begins to make sense. But because we are so busy in blocking the uncomfortable emotions, we stay hung in that uncertain state for almost forever. But not anymore, as we are now getting to know the true meaning of **just being**.

Now "Being in the Moment" makes total sense. While we were thinking that being in the moment is to focus on the external actions that we do, the true meaning of being in the moment is to just allow ourselves every moment to feel what we feel.

Always remember, that inside us reside two people (The mind and the feelings). For every situation in our lives, a conversation takes place between these two people. Where the feelings speak about how they feel currently, the mind tries to make the individual feel guilty for feeling that way and mind is nothing but a collection of all that has been observed by the sensory perceptions and tries to bring logic and social acceptance to everything and stops the free flow of current emotions.

This mind which does not have a mind of its own but is just a collection of memory (Situation + Feeling associated with that Situation) tries to limit the expansive nature of the being. This will now put the individual into the state of Resistance. Now one will start to pretend as if the initial feeling that they felt should not be given preference to.

But if you observe carefully, every time feelings precede and then comes the Mind with its collection of limited logic to either amplify or reject the feeling. So if you see the nature of a being, it is always feeling first. This answers the question itself, what should precede?

Resistance is like ignoring the hunger and thinking that a spoon of nuts or peanut butter would be enough and eventually end up eating small bits and bites throughout the day as the stomach is constantly signaling that it needs proper attention with enough food. Instead if we had sat down and had a proper meal, then at least the time between two meal would have been more useful and productive rather than constantly thinking and feeling the hunger and munching on small bites thinking there is no time or no need for a meal.

Resistance is like knowing that there is a small piece of paper or anything lying on the floor but still walking around it, jumping over it but avoid picking it up and throwing it in the bin. Or placing it back to where it was. Will give examples to understand this better.

This is a scenario where a person for some unknown reason does not feel like opening the window in the room for 5 minutes of ventilation (which otherwise was done every day).So now the conversation between the feeling and mind begins:

Feeling : I am not going to open the window of the room.

Mind   : But you do it every day.

Feeling : Yeah I know but not today.

Mind   : This will slowly stop you from being disciplined. Better to do it.

Feeling : But I feel too pressurized sometimes with the daily routine. I need a break.

Mind   : But you just opened the window of other rooms, then how long is it going to take to
open one more window?

Feeling : Hmmm, this is not done. One day of break looks like impossible……

Mind   : Yeah, that's life. Just do it.

Feeling : You know what, I will not. So hey you mind do not try to trap me in guilt.

Mind   : ....

After two minutes: The Person goes and opens the window of the room BUT this time with no feeling of "pressure", with no "stress"......why?

It is because the person took the power back from the mind, but how?

When the person stood by what was felt, the mind at that point went blank as it did not have anything to counter back. The feelings felt respected, addressed to and stopped bothering the person. This refreshed the person and then the person opened the window by their own choice and not because of the guilt trap that the mind tried to set up based on limited logic. By the way this whole scenario happened within five minutes.

The next scenario is about making their bed:

Feeling : I will do it after I am back home in an hour.
Mind   : What about the rule that is popular "Make your bed as the first thing in the morning and you will feel a sense of completion".
Feeling : Yes, I know about this but today I need to give my attention to something else first.
Mind   : Well you are slowly giving up too many things. This is not good.
Feeling : I am making this choice consciously and I know that this is not about giving up.
Mind   : ....

The person steps out with no guilt nor regret. Finishes the outside task, comes home, makes the bed and the state of feeling is "Calm" Why and How?

The answer remains the same. The person took the power back from the mind. Made the decision with full awareness and stood by what was decided.
This conversation happened within 30 seconds.

Now before I proceed with the next scenarios, I would like to give some more insight into this topic.

Given a choice between Mind and Feeling, go for Feeling.

Mind is nothing but a collection of all that a person has experienced and absorbed from the outer surroundings and

Mind cannot exist on its own. It needs input or some kind of feed through the five senses (6th Sense will activate only when the person works towards it by **just being**). Feelings on the other hand are original in nature. Nobody till date created a feeling, all what the evolution did is to give a name to a particular feeling like anxiety, nervousness, happiness, calmness, fear, agitation, anger, sadness, peacefulness and the list goes on. So to become the authentic self, one has to choose Authenticity and to do this the 'Feeling' holds the top position in authenticity as it is original in nature.

Having said this, I am sure people who are reading this book are clear enough to know that while giving priority to feeling one has to remember the ethical behaviour. Also the emphasis is made on Feeling it internally. Which means no thing or living being should be attacked or hurt physically in this process.

"Solution" is not the same as what "we want the solution to look like" in a situation. Hence often it so happens that we do not allow the solution to flow through and rather place "what we want the solution to look like" in the way. It is like standing in a parking area and then waving hand to the car approaching to park it there. Now how will someone park the car when you are standing right on that parking area?

Now let us proceed with the next set of scenarios where the person allowed the mind to take higher priority.

This is a scenario where every time a parent (who has lost their spouse and lives alone) visits their child (who has their own family now) and on the day of leaving from their child's place a particular conversation takes place.

Parent : Our next generation is selfish.

Child : Why do you say so?

Parent : They do not have an emotional maturity. They do not think about their immediate others. Money fascinates them and they leave their parents alone and travel to different cities and countries for their own benefit.

Child : Ok, but it sometimes gets difficult to find a job in the same city.

Parent : This is just an excuse. One can get it if they want to. The children want to go away and that is reason they find job somewhere else.

Child : At times yes because the pressure from the family and relatives feel suffocating.

Parent : This does not mean that one runs away from responsibilities.

Child : What responsibilities are you taking about. Have I not done anything for you ?

Parent : My friend's child took them to a world tour. Bought my friend a new home.

And in this manner the conversation gets heated up, the Parent later that day leaves for their home. If we closely observe this conversation it is actually about a **different** feeling which is spoken in a **masked** form. Let us **decode** it.

The parent here is actually feeling lonely. As the day to depart approaches, the parent is sensing that the loneliness will be felt once again. Let us read the internal conversation that takes place between the parent's Mind and Feeling.

Feeling : Once again loneliness hmmmm.

Mind : That's life, you are not the only one who is facing this.

Feeling : Yeah but how nice it would be if I get to see my child more often and spend more time. The food is also great here. It feels nice to have meals together.

Mind : You cannot show how you feeling to your child. The world will laugh at you for being vulnerable. You need show that you are strong.

Feeling : I feel suppressed if I am unable to feel it.

Mind : It is a tough pill but you have to swallow it.

Feeling : I feel like extending the stay but feel embarrassed at the same time.

Mind : Just put up a mask of strength.

Feeling : It is getting tougher to hide the pain of loneliness.

In this manner the parent starts to resist what is being felt under the worldly pressure which is constantly being reminded of by the mind. The child on the other hand is unable to decode it at first and then later understands that it is the parent's loneliness speaking but knows that it cannot be openly asked in front of the parent.

How would the conversation look like, if each one allowed the feelings to be felt and addressed them by "Just Being".

Parent : I am going to miss you all so much.
Child : We will miss you as well. Staying alone must be hard.
Parent : Yeah at times it is good, as it gives me my space but the rest of the time I miss companionship. Eating meals together feels way better than alone.
Child : Oh by the way, I have packed few boxes with your favourite snacks and meals.
Parent : Yey That feels so awesome to know that I have stock of delicious food.
Child : Do you want to join some group activities conducted for Senior Citizens?
Parent : Yeah sounds interesting but I am not that comfortable to check it online and make the booking. Can you help me here?
Child : I have already checked few programs and we can shortlist them together. Also let us plan our next meet.

In this way both are being their authentic self and the end result is - Solution to the loneliness.

Often in the process of trying to be someone or something else than the true authentic, we lose the essence of the conversation. It becomes so indirect that it eventually ends up in misunderstanding. The current Social pressure is mightier than we can imagine. Everything is measured based upon how famous it is, or how many people are doing it or what value it holds in others opinion. To be authentic has become the most difficult thing on this planet.

Life has become a race and rather than living the life, we are running in a race which is a maze of illusion. Why did I call it illusion ? If you observe it clearly there is no end point to this. One cannot clearly define that the winner of this race will feel "Contended, Satisfied and will be in Bliss".

Study, Earn and keep earning, buy materialistic things and the list keeps expanding and then to fulfill that list, keep running in this maze. One does not even enjoy the fruits of their hard work. Where during a vacation, there is an image capturing device between the person and the scenery. It has become all about posting it on the social media and showing it to an invisible and non-existent community. And the best part is, this invisible community is least interested in anyone's happiness and rather wants to mimic and do things that others do.

None lives in the moment. Mind has its eyes on the future and feelings are ignored for being authentic as they become a hinderance for the mind.

Life is to live, that's it. While living, we look inside us through the eyes of the feeling. We know how a machine works much better than the "best designed machine ever" which is our "Human Being".

Everything about "Being" is ignored.

Most of us would not know the rhythm of our heart beat. If for once we shift our focus inward by listening to what the feeling is trying to communicate to us, we will never feel lonely. The feeling is the best companion we could ever get in our life. It is the best navigator of our "Journey" called "Life". It knows when to talk to us and when to ask us to rest.

Of course we have our duties toward our family, our society and our planet. But in this we forget the duty towards oneself which is "Just being" and the rest will be taken care of.

Feeling says "Sit Down " and we "Run".

Feeling says "Eat" and we say " Diet".

Feeling says " Rest" and we say "I will be considered indisciplined if I sleep for a little longer".

Feeling says " Stretch your body" and we say " Weight lifting".

Feeling says "Live" and we say "Run behind the non-existent".

Do you want to know what life is ?

It is to live that moment with full attention. When I say full attention, it could be any feeling. The point is to just feel it to the fullest.

Think for a moment. Earning, Investing, Stressing about expanding the wealth, running after it for countless sleepless nights and then once all that has been achieved, then what next ?

So much of hard work and planning for what ? Nothing isn't it?

Instead, attending to one's feeling and to feel it to the fullest will be the best solution to everything. There is not ultimate goal in life other than "Just Being".

"Just Being" is the ultimate destination.

"Just Be" till the last breath of life. This is what is called "Meditation".

Byproduct : This state of being will automatically allow great ideas, solutions, good health and abundance in life. It will give you more than what was expected.

The Wet Feet Concept :

Let us imagine that we have wet our feet in water.

Now we get a pair of socks and try to wear them on our wet feet.

Can you imagine the struggle it takes to wear it on wet feet but we still continue to pull and push and somehow get them on our feet.

What would have been a better option? Well it is obvious that, it would have been easier to wipe the feet first, and then wear the socks on.

This is exactly what we are doing with our lives. The wet feet symbolize the feelings (Point A). The cloth with which we wipe our feet is similar to we paying attention to these feelings (Point B). The Socks represent the place where we want to reach (Point C).

Hence if we try to jump from Point A to Point C without focusing on Point B, the loss is ours.

Point B will help us get there where we wish to be. This point B is all about just being.

The Skin Moisturizer :

It is said that applying the skin moisturizer (natural oil) immediately after the bath gives best results. So why is it so ?

There could be several reasons but from a lay man's perspective we have experienced that the moisturizer spreads easily and evenly without much effort when applied just after bath and the skin feels soft almost instantly. Which means that the same wet or moist feet made it difficult for the socks to be worn, but helped in softening and nourishing the skin when it came to applying the moisturizer.

Here the skin moisturizer is referring to : Taking care of once feelings immediately or at the earliest would heal the person from that situation sooner and in a much easier way because we did not allow the feelings to be rejected, we did not resist it and hence the feelings did neither multiply itself nor did it go that deep inside us to affect our health or life drastically.

The Examination in School :

When we write our exams in the school, the questions are a combination of easy ,moderate and really tough ones. Also to avoid copying, they have different set of question papers distributed among the students.

All we do is to try and solve them. At the least attempt every question. There is no emotion attached to the question paper. We see the questions as they are. Which means if they are easy then we see them as easy, If moderate then we see them as moderate and if tough then we see them as tough.

Then why is it that life is expected to be easy and only easy and why is it that we look at someone else's life and wish for that to be ours. This life is same as a school.

Based on our deeds and actions the circumstances appear. Instead of living them, we judge them (which is a normal human behaviour) and create a sense of resistance.

If we face a tough situation, we have the complete authority to feel upset about it, cry and feel weak and disheartened. But instead of feeling these true emotions, we try to talk ourselves out of it by saying that feeling low is sign of a weak person and that why does this happen to me and not to others or how comfortable is the life of other people. The truth though is something very different.

The truth is that every feeling and emotion should be seen as a fact as they are. Nothing is above or below anything. They are similar to the syllabus in school where they try to have maximum coverage of subjects. Life is a much more sophisticated school system where each one gets different syllabus and definitely unique question paper. There is nothing left to compare our life with others because their question paper is altogether a different one.

If we learn how to solve and find solution to those questions then we are promoted to next class in this "School of Life" and if not then we will have to repeat the same class. This is the reason that similar situation arises several times in life through different people or places. Once we learn to "Just Be" and observe the feeling that this situation creates or activates, then we understand the lesson to be learnt from it. That particular pattern cannot repeat as we have found the answer to that question.

So if we are still comparing our lives with that of others, and measuring the importance of our being based upon these comparisons, then we should also be ready to have all the experiences which that other person is having, which could also mean that whoever compares themselves with that other, should be prepared to also die on the same day at the same time like that other person.

What I am trying to say is that, it is time we realize everyone's life has different patterns, different lessons to be learned and different timeline when it comes to their physical existence on this planet.

At times we can with years of experience learn to categorize and group certain people who have similar patterns in life but we cannot be sure that there exist only these many kind of people or patterns.

So what does this point us to : Start to live life by "Just being" rather than trying to become "like other human being".

So Just being at Point B will take us to where we need to go. Also so far I said that it will take us to Point C. But who knows by Just being at Point B, It might take us to the unseen Points like D,E,K,L,S and so on. Where we thought that Point C is the best for us, it could actually help us see that may be we need to go to Point S and not Point C.

HOW DOES "JUST BEING" HELP US LIVE THE LIFE TO ITS FULLEST :

Common Sense is the most uncommon tool that we have used.

What is called as the "sixth sense", or "higher intuition" or "gut feeling" or "highly sensitive beings" is to my understanding nothing but the "Common Sense".

We have been provided with the most sophisticated tool called "Common Sense" and we ignore it the most.

So by "Just being" we empty our storage tank by feeling the feeling and addressing it.

Once it is emptied or some space is created, then we are a little more focused on the current moment. This means we are more aware of our inner and outer surroundings at that present moment. In short we are "Present". Once we are present, then we think better, the response time is quick and at the same time effective. The byproduct of which is great and effective ideas and sensible solution to that situation. This is termed as Common Sense.

Let us read an example to understand it further:

Guests arrive and the host offers to make tea for them.

While preparing the tea, the host looks for milk and finds out that it is empty.

Host is relaxed and thinks of how it can be replaced. In that moment, the host remembers that there is Milk powder at home. Adds it to the tea, and the guest relish it with joy.

What just happened : The host was fully present (in the moment) in that scenario and the so called common sense (which is also the presence of mind) got activated and the idea of milk powder flashed in and helped the situation.

The same scenario could have turned out totally different if the host was already filled up with many ignored and suppressed feelings. Reason being, the host would have been pre occupied and filled up with overload of unprocessed feelings and would have had no energy left to act upon the current scenario. So instead of thinking in the direction of solution, the host would have thought in the direction of guilt, anger and shame. The host would have felt upset about the promise of tea which cannot be offered, or would have rushed to the food market to buy some milk and had it been after the food market was closed, then would have felt helpless and dejected.

Hence if we are regular in being at Point B, the rest of the world falls in place because our way of living life will become solution oriented.

This is how the people have come up with great ideas in life which we think of as an impossible task to achieve and that it is reserved for the 0.1% of the people. But in reality we all can have this and much more, provided we learn to remember the Point B.

Point B under the Microscope

Let us dive deeper into this concept.
Suppose someone hurt us in some way. It could be by lying to us or leaving us. It could also be by being disrespectful to us and so on.

Feeling : I feel hurt and angry at the same time.
Mind : Well that is how world is, move on.
Feeling : I am unable to move on ,the pain is too much.
Mind : If you choose to be a loser, then carry on with this heavy heart. No one cares.
Feeling : No one cares and that hurts. At the least I can care for myself and I regret not doing that.
Mind : Well they are the ones who did this to you, so why so do you have to suffer, get up and be strong.
Feeling : Yes they are the ones who did this to me, but I cannot just instantly feel happy and move on. It takes time. I feel being pushed too hard to feel different too soon.
Mind : You are wasting your time. Grow up. Show them that you do not care for them.
Feeling : Well I still do care and I cannot fake.
Mind : May be what they did you was for your good, they were not worth your companionship.
Feeling : You might be right but I miss their companionship and it hurts at the same time.
Mind : How about you take a vacation, spend some money on great things. Buy the expensive things and it might feel like you have pampered yourself.

Feeling : For me the best pampering would be to be in the loved ones company, have a good meal together and be comfortable in those soft Pajamas which are several years old.

Mind : well hmmm…..

Feeling : Let me take my time. I do not know the reason why it happened. It might make sense later but as of now I am feeling a lot of pain and hurt and this is my current Truth. Let it change in future but for now I cannot jump into any other feeling.

Mind:……………………………………………..

So as you read this conversation, you will see that the Person tried to be at Point B. This practice will help an individual connect with their core. Since the feeling was given its space and was given an ear to listen to, the person will be able to for at least the next few hours focus on the work or anything that needs the single pointed attention.

The hurt and pain might pop up several times for several days but the intensity will reduce and after a while, the person will recollect the situation that happened but will notice that there is no feeling attached to it. Now the person is just observing the situation which took place in the past and no triggers are felt. With this one can understand the phrase "Observe your thoughts like the flowing water".

This happens only when we feel the intensity that is supposed to be felt, and then all that remains is a registry of an event that happened in life and no feelings attached to them.

When someone dies, a mourning period is observed ? why is it so ? why can it not be like, Ok so and so died. Do the death ritual and then just get up the next day and go to work and get back to routine. It is the release of Soul from the body so just chill. Do you think we will be able to do this although we know in theory that it is true, that Soul is now set free to move ahead.

Mourning period is for the human body to slowly come out of this energy exchange which it had with this person who died. There are so many habits and routines that could have been shared among the two. This takes time.

Now if the person thinks of this deceased person after a year, the pain exists and may be tears too but the person is able to come out of that feeling a bit faster.

In this way when a decade goes by and the person thinks of this deceased person, it is just the event that happened. Might feel a slight pinch in the heart but it is close to just observing the event with almost no feelings attached to it.

Give yourself the time it needs to cope up with any situation. When I say give time it could mean a whole lifetime or several lifetimes as well. The best part is that ,it will heal sooner than we thought because now the feeling feels welcome and where there is no resistance ,there is free flow and things work faster. This is called flowing in the direction of water rather than swimming against the direction of water flow.

Unplug

What does mind store and how is it stored ?

Mind stores all experiences of the life and it can only store them when that experience has an unprocessed feeling attached to it.

For example a situation takes place which made you feel uncomfortable. You resisted this uncomfortable feeling and tried to do the other things in life. Now Mind will label that situation with the feeling "uncomfortable" and store it under that label.

Similarly a situation that made you sad and you resisted that sad feeling, the mind will pick this situation and label it with " Sadness" and store it under that label.

Hence the storage structure of mind is purely label based derived from unprocessed feelings.

The next time when one feels sad, mind will immediately flash before this person some of the situations that had a high intensity of "Sadness" attached to it and a domino effect of sadness begins to dominate this person.

How would it have helped by being at "Point B" immediately?

By being at Point B we will be able to unplug this situation from that feeling by actually feeling it to the fullest. It is like a bottle filled with some water or juice and when we drink it fully, then all that is left is empty bottle which is either disposed or sent to the recycle system. Similarly now all that is left is the memory of that situation and mind will remove it from the storage folder which is labelled "Sadness" and place it in a folder named "unknown" or "For Future reference". This is called unplugging.

So the more we stay at Point B and address that feeling at the earliest and feel it to its fullest, then that situation loses the attachment to that feeling and all that is left is a trace of that situation which goes under the "unknown" folder.

This folder with the label "unknown" when opened for some reason, will not trigger any feeling but will just display the images of that situation. We will just observe it as a movie that's it. For example looking at the photo album of some person or scene, will just be an image and nothing will pinch the heart.

The folder with the label "For Future reference" will get opened when we see a situation repeating in life and then we pull this from our stored memory to remind ourselves to learn from the past and not repeat it but it will not create chaos and rather would be like a helping tool.

There are some labels which are ok to have and they are the labels of happiness, joy, peace, bliss. But in the path of spirituality, these labels will also slow down the progress.

If we do not practice Just being at Point B, then the mind will continue the storage of these situations(with unprocessed feelings) and if the storage is full, it will start storing them in our organs, muscles, bones and so on which will then show up as illness and diseases.

Just being at Point B is not easy for sure. Especially when it makes us feel uneasy or uncomfortable. Now before I explain the different stages of being at Point B, let me tell you that generally all the unprocessed feelings have an uncomfortable feeling attached to it. Anything that works in our favour or is a pleasant experience would add on to the ego or pride or self-worth but does not bother nor does it feel uncomfortable enough for it to hinder.

The five stages of being at Point B

1.   <u>Nothing Changes</u> :

Initially the person just feels it but it does not make the person think that something should be changed here, or there is a lesson that needs to be leant from this. It is at a very initial stage of just being felt. And it is absolutely ok. This is how it starts.

2.   <u>The Outside Should Change:</u>

The next stage is where the person feels that the outside which gave this uncomfortable feeling should change. The outside should take the re-sponsibility of changing itself. After a while the person realizes that changing the outside is an il-lusion.

3.   <u>Contemplate on it</u>:

The next stage is to deeply ponder over what hap-pened and re run the scenario and see why and what happened. Why is the outside not being re-sponsible and changing itself ? Why are there such kind of people who do not care about others ? why is the world becoming more self-centered ? Why me ?

4.   <u>Give up</u>:

There comes the next stage where it feels like too much of inner work for no result.

There is fatigue and the person gives up.

5.   <u>Change from Within</u>:

Now the person reaches the final stage where the realization comes in that the change has to happen from within. Often change from within is disliked by most or all because without doing anything wrong, when one needs to change and the outside remains the same, it triggers anger. But the true meaning of changing from within is very different from what we perceived about it. Changing from within means , that our thought process is now "Solution Oriented". The Solution could be bringing a change in routine, or leaving a situation, it could mean removing or adding something in life etc. Let us know this better by reading some examples.

Example 1:

The classic social media example. This has created a havoc in lives of many. This has become the new scale of measurement for happiness and success in life or even the for the basic right to live. The display of fancy life, expensive vacations, being forever online on social media platforms, and higher the quantity of online posts of personal life, the better the life. Every moment of life is first witnessed by the image capturing device (be it phone, tablet, laptop, camera, drones and what not) and it has gone to an extend that even a newborn's blur vision would at first see this device because the parent must be capturing the birth. This craziness has created an illusion in people's life that everything has to be larger than life, the celebrations are for others and for online viewers. After several attempts of sadness, disappointment with one's life by comparing with outer online world, finally some set of people are starting to understand that "the change has to happen from within" by going offline and connecting to the real world, to avoid posting on social media, trying to connect more to the nature and actually having a life close to nature, turning the television off and rather go on a walk or read some useful hardbound books, reduce the screentime and so on. Rather than allowing the machines to do the household activities while one uses that time for watching irrelevant and illusionary stuff, it is better to do the household activities and feel connected to the true life. This is still an ongoing process and will take forever for some to understand what actually needs to change.

Example 2 :

Relationship. With time, people slowly get to see that the opposite person is not what they actually thought to be. When situations of pain, tragedy happen is when people understand that their choices were wrong. So initially people feel the hurt, and then want the opposite to change their behaviour, and then knowing that the opposite is not going to change their behaviour, people start to contemplate on the decision, then gives up and say this is life and life is not good. Finally a moment enters where the true reason for all what happened reveals itself. finally people start to walk on the path of solution, taking the power back and not being trapped anymore. This can take a lifetime of being at Point B and that is ok.

Example 3:

The fit in syndrome. This is faced by almost everyone since childhood. Almost everyone tries to fit in
to a group be it school, college, work, family or society. There are people who feel suffocated early
enough in life when trying to fit in but then they
do not understand it initially. They start with the
sad feeling that nobody wants them in their life.
Then they want the outside to change. Then comes
the phase of contemplation of why me ? The life
seems to be dull and lonely (The give up stage).
Finally the " Change from Within" happens where
the source of "need to fit in" gets revealed. The
source could be parents, neighbours , school and
all those who contribute to the way a person sees
the world. Now the person gets onto to the un-
learning phase and tries to rework on the mindset.
Hence the solution oriented path is finally been
chosen. Slowly but surely there will be a day
where the need to fit in will vanish.

These were just some basic examples, but the reader
must have by this time understood the different stages of
being at Point B and that "Changing from Within" is actually liberating. It gives you the solution which helps to take
the power back.

To Let Go:

The True meaning of " To Let Go" is To "Change From Within". To let go does not mean that we have to accept the unjust acts and behaviours nor does it mean that we forget the situation. It does not mean that we have to forgive the opposite. All it means is "to let go" of the problem by thinking Solution oriented and as mentioned earlier the Solution is what you think is best for you based upon the analysis.

<u>This process of Changing from Within can be enhanced by</u>:
-Writing those feelings.
-Having a self-talk.
-Saying No and staying away from situations and people physically if and when possible.
-Speaking to friends if you are sure that they can be trusted.
-Expressing the feelings when in alone. Like literally having a conversation by speaking it aloud to oneself so that what is being felt is spoken through the Mouth and heard by the Ears, which will help understand the feelings better.
-Talking to Professional listeners.
Initially all these things will look like a huge effort but very soon it will become a routine to stay at Point B.

Cure is Better Than Prevention

We have always heard that prevention is better than cure but in this case the reverse of it works best. The more you prevent (which means the more you resist the current feeling) the worse it will get. Hence Cure which is "just being at Point B" will automatically take you to Point C and remember that Point C can be different for different people.

Miscellaneous

<u>The Empath's Inside out</u> :

Let us understand it with an example.

Person A : Hi , how are you ?

Person B : I am good, just came here to the shop during my lunch break.

Person A : that's nice to have the office close to the shopping area.

Person B : Yeah , I am looking for a pair of comfortable jeans for my kid but I am unable to find them in this shop. I have to get back to work as the lunch break is over. Was nice to meet you here. Bye.

Person A : Bye.

The empath inside Person A : I have some time today, how about I go to the other shop and buy that jeans that this Person B was looking for and give it this evening.

Analysis : Although it does not seem like a big deal to buy it, it is indeed a big deal. Person B never asked for any help. Person B is fully capable of buying it on their own.

This is how Person A will invest the energy in going over the board every time and exhaust oneself. There is difference between help and extreme help. So for all the empaths out there, evaluate your decision of helping every time when the empath inside you tries to go on the path of Extreme help.

<u>**The Alarm concept**</u>:

We set the alarm so that it will wake us up on time and when it actually does its job by ringing on time, we get angry on it and turn it off.

Similarly when we were going to be born, we decided that in this lifetime these are the set of lessons we would learn and these are the set of things that we shall do. Then we ask the Soul to tell/remind the physical body of the tasks.

Now life happens and the Soul rings the Alarm, how ? through some situation that happens in life but with less intensity. Unknowingly we press the snooze button and continue to repeat the patterns in life. After sometime, The alarm rings with a much more louder tone. We still ignore, and walk on the path of illusion. Finally the alarm rings so loud (Tough situation in life) which then makes us think and rework and restart life but this time for the Soul's purpose.

Remember that Life is a Journey and It cannot be Mastered because this journey will always have a combination of known and unknown situations. Hence instead of investing energy in mastering something which cannot be mastered, it is better to master the art of "Just Being" at Point B and it will tell us which is our next stop in this Journey of Life.

Wishing You All An Authentic
Experience At Point B.

Thank You